D0637059

GALILEO! GALILEO!

TO APRIL -- ARCHIVIST, ARCHITECT, APIARIST, FRIEND

OTHER BOOKS BY THE AUTHORS :

ESME DOOLEY

ESME DOOLEY & THE KIRKKOMAKI CIRCUS

GALILEO! GALILEO!

WRITTEN AND ILLUSTRATED BY

HOLLY TRECHTER AND JANE DONOVAN

SKY CANDLE PRESS

ZUMBRO FALLS, MINNESOTA

GALILEO! GALILEO!

COPYRIGHT © 2020 BY HOLLY TRECHTER AND JANE DONOVAN

PUBLISHED 2020 BY SKY CANDLE PRESS
PRINTED IN THE UNITED STATES OF AMERICA

ALL RIGHTS RESERVED. NO PART OF THIS BOOK MAY BE USED OR REPRODUCED IN ANY MANNER WHATSOEVER WITHOUT WRITTEN PERMISSION EXCEPT IN THE CASE OF BRIEF QUOTATIONS EMBODIED IN CRITICAL ARTICLES AND REVIEWS. FOR INFORMATION, PLEASE ADDRESS SKY CANDLE PRESS, ZUMBRO FALLS, MN 55991.

MOST OF THIS BOOK IS A WORK OF NONFICTION. SOME OF THE PLACES AND CHARACTERS ARE PRODUCTS OF THE AUTHORS' IMAGINATIONS; RESEMBLANCES TO ACTUAL PLACES OR PERSONS ARE COINCIDENTAL. INCLUSION OF PAST OR PRESENT PUBLIC FIGURES DOES NOT IMPLY THEIR ENDORSEMENT OF THIS BOOK.

NASA HAS NOT EXPRESSED OR IMPLIED ENDORSEMENT OR SPONSORSHIP OF THIS PROJECT.

FIRST EDITION
ISBN 978-1-939360-08-3
LIBRARY OF CONGRESS CONTROL NUMBER: 2020900969

MY NAME IS GALILEO, AND SOME PEOPLE SAY I CHANGED THE WORLD.

YOU SEE, I BUILT A POWERFUL TELESCOPE,
AND ONE NIGHT I TURNED IT TOWARDS JUPITER.

THAT WAS IN ITALY, IN 1610.
BUT MAYBE YOU ALREADY GUESSED THAT FROM MY VERY STYLISH CLOTHES!
ANYWAY, I WATCHED FOR A FEW NIGHTS, AND THEN A FOURTH STAR POPPED OUT BY JUPITER.
HI!
AND THAT'S WHEN IT HIT ME.
THEY'RE NOT STARS, THEY'RE MOONS!

BACK THEN, MOST PEOPLE BELIEVED THAT EVERYTHING REVOLVED AROUND THE EARTH.
SO I SHOCKED THEM WHEN I SAID MOONS WERE REVOLVING AROUND JUPITER.
Jupiter
Saturn
Sun
Venus
Mars
Moon
Mercury
They thought Earth was the center of everything.
Earth
USING MY TELESCOPE, I ALSO SAW SPOTS ON THE SUN AND CRATERS ON OUR MOON. THIS ALARMED PEOPLE TOO BECAUSE THEY THOUGHT HEAVENLY BODIES WERE SUPPOSED TO BE PERFECT.
YOU LOOK MARVELOUS.
NO, YOU LOOK MARVELOUS.

I WAS MAKING POWERFUL PEOPLE NERVOUS, SO THE INQUISITION HAULED ME IN FOR A TRIAL.
THEY CLAIMED I HAD UNACCEPTABLE BELIEFS.
SERIOUSLY?
YES, SERIOUSLY.
GUILTY!
GUILTY!
GUILTY!
THEY PLACED ME UNDER HOUSE ARREST FOR THE REST OF MY LIFE. IT WAS A HARD WAY TO SPEND MY FINAL YEARS.
MAMA MIA.

I'M SORRY TO SAY THAT IN 1642, I DIED. ON THE BRIGHT SIDE, IT FREED ME UP FOR OTHER THINGS.

THEY COULDN'T TELL, BECAUSE ALL THEIR SCIENTIFIC INSTRUMENTS WERE STUCK ON EARTH. IF ONLY THEY WERE CLOSER TO MYSTERIOUS JUPITER...

SO NASA (THE NATIONAL AERONAUTICS AND SPACE ADMINISTRATION) BEGAN TO THINK ABOUT A JUPITER MISSION.

...AFTER WORLD WAR II, GERMAN SCIENTISTS WERE BROUGHT TO THE UNITED STATES TO KEEP THEIR SKILLS AWAY FROM GERMANY AND THE SOVIET UNION.

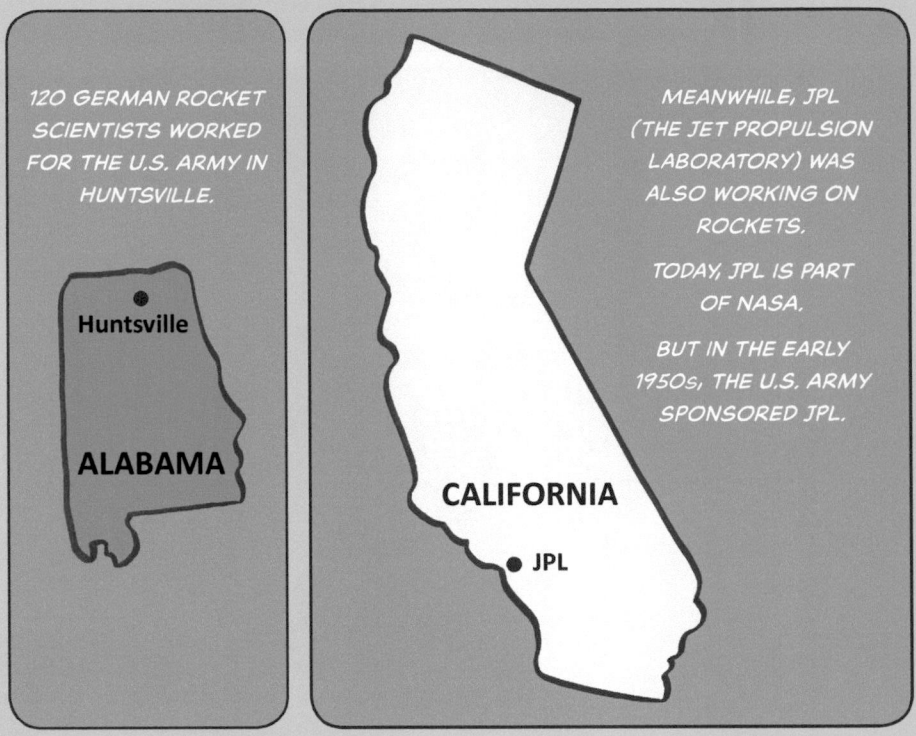

THEY FORMED GOOD RELATIONSHIPS WHICH WOULD HELP NASA WHEN IT STARTED IN 1958.

TIME PASSED, AND THE WORLD GREW FASCINATED WITH SPACE TRAVEL.

IN 1974, THE UNITED STATES AND GERMANY DECIDED TO WORK TOGETHER ON A JUPITER MISSION.

FOR THE JOP PROJECT, THE ENGINEERS WANTED TO BUILD A SPINNING SPACECRAFT BECAUSE THEY THOUGHT IT WOULD BE MORE STABLE IF IT SPUN.

SO THE ENGINEERS CAME UP WITH A CLEVER DESIGN.

THE SPACECRAFT WILL SPIN.
BUT WE'LL BUILD IT IN A WAY THAT WILL LET US PAUSE THE CAMERAS LONG ENOUGH TO SNAP A PICTURE.
Fast antenna
SAY "CHEESE."
Probe
Camera
BY 1976, THE JOP MISSION PLAN WAS SETTLED.
OUR SPACECRAFT WILL DROP A PROBE INTO JUPITER'S ATMOSPHERE.
AFTER THAT, IT WILL ORBIT JUPITER FOR TWO YEARS, TO COLLECT DATA.
Probe

THE ENGINEERS KEPT WORKING. BEFORE LONG, IT WAS 1977.

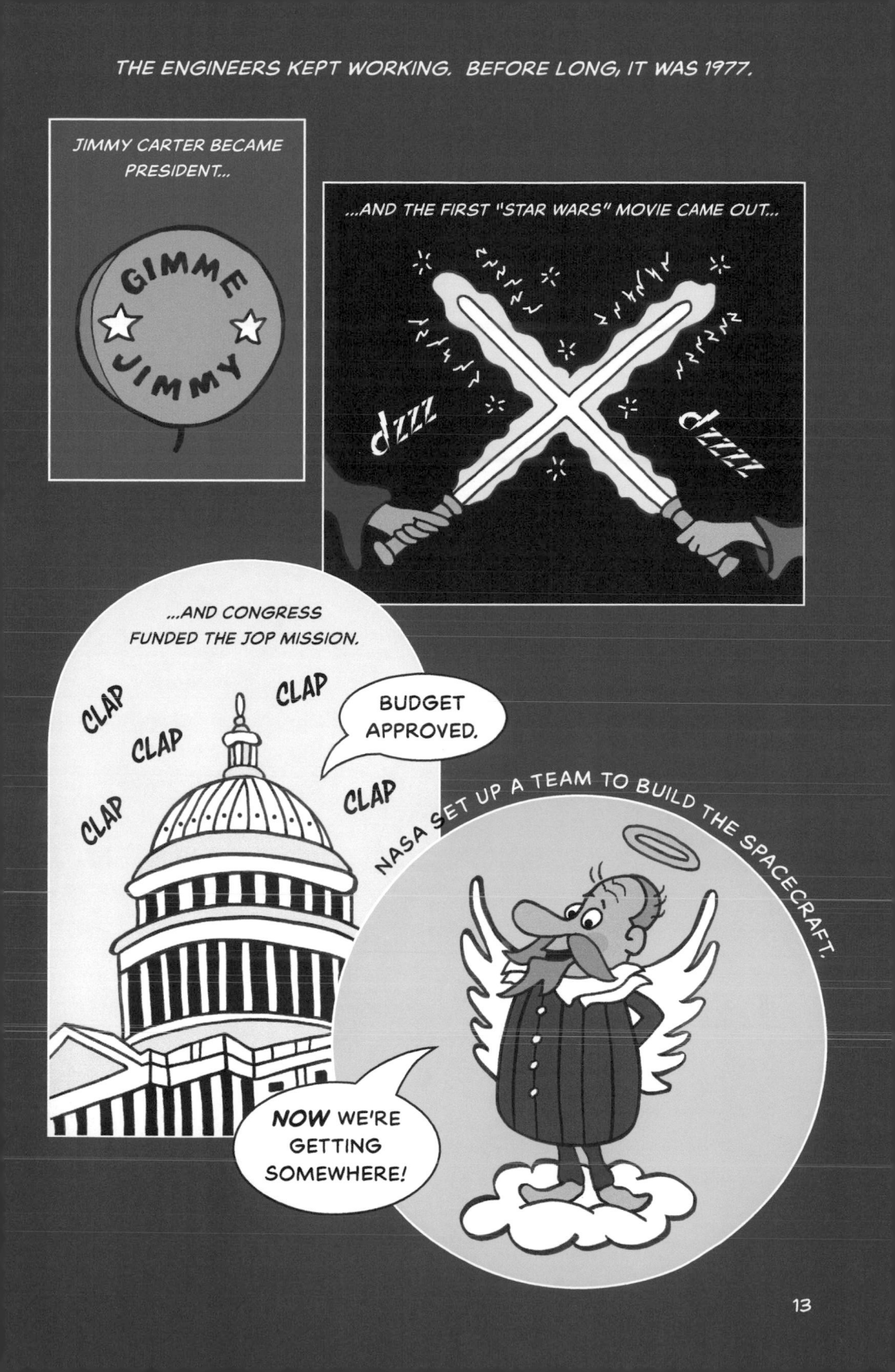

FIRST WE NEED TO COME UP WITH A BETTER MISSION NAME. "JOP" IS SO BLAH.
Maximus?
Magellan?
Pete?
Columbus?
WELL, HOW ABOUT CALLING IT "GALILEO?" AFTER ALL, HE DISCOVERED JUPITER'S MOONS.
AND THAT'S HOW THE "GALILEO" MISSION WAS BORN.
I LOVE IT!

THE AMERICANS AND THEIR GERMAN PARTNERS ON THE GALILEO MISSION HAD TO FIGURE OUT WHO WOULD BE DOING WHAT.

SHOULD WE USE A ROCKET TO BLAST GALILEO INTO SPACE?
OR SHOULD WE USE THE NEW SPACE SHUTTLE? IT'S ABOUT READY.
THIS WAS IN THE EARLY DAYS OF THE SHUTTLE PROGRAM, WHEN THINGS WEREN'T EXACTLY WORKING SMOOTHLY.
WHAP
THAT'S GOTTA HURT.

THE GALILEO TEAM WENT BACK AND FORTH, TRYING TO DECIDE BETWEEN A ROCKET AND THE SHUTTLE.
OR
THE ROCKET WOULD BE A ONE-SHOT DEAL.
AFTER THE LAUNCH, ITS PARTS WOULD FALL AWAY, AND WE WOULDN'T BE ABLE TO USE THEM AGAIN.
THE SHUTTLE, ON THE OTHER HAND, WOULD BE REUSABLE.
WE COULD FLY IT UP HIGH AND PUSH GALILEO OUT OF ITS CARGO HOLD. THEN THE SHUTTLE COULD COME BACK TO EARTH.
ALSO, THERE WAS ANOTHER PART TO THE PUZZLE...

...NASA FEARED THAT PEOPLE WOULDN'T GET EXCITED ABOUT THE MISSION IF IT DIDN'T HAVE ASTRONAUTS.
THE SHUTTLE NEEDS SOMEONE LIKE ME TO FLY IT. MAYBE THE PUBLIC WOULD BE INTERESTED IN THAT.
BUT THE SPACE SHUTTLE IS SO EXPENSIVE.
JUST WAIT, IT WILL GET CHEAPER.
IT WAS A TOUGH DECISION.

NASA FINALLY DECIDED TO USE THE SPACE SHUTTLE TO LAUNCH GALILEO.

THEY HAD NO IDEA HOW HARD IT WAS GOING TO BE.

BUT THE SHUTTLE PROGRAM KEPT HAVING PROBLEMS.

SO THEY POSTPONED GALILEO'S LAUNCH FOR TWO YEARS, TO GIVE THE SHUTTLE A CHANCE TO CATCH UP.

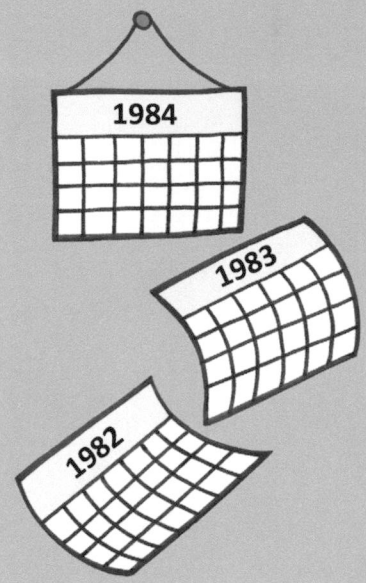

MAYBE WE SHOULDN'T HAVE CHOSEN THE SHUTTLE FOR GALILEO.

BUT WE CAN'T BACK OUT NOW. THE SHUTTLE CAN'T LOSE A CARGO AS IMPORTANT AS GALILEO.

AS THE GALILEO TEAM WAITED FOR THEIR SHUTTLE RIDE, THEY WORKED ON WHAT THEY CALLED THE "UPPER STAGE."

TIME PASSED.
IT WAS NOW 1981.
RUBIK'S CUBES WERE IN TOY STORES ACROSS THE COUNTRY...
CLICKETY
CLICK
...AND THE FIRST SPACE SHUTTLE LAUNCHED...
WE'LL TAKE GALILEO UP ON A FUTURE FLIGHT.
USA
RUMBLE
...AND RONALD REAGAN BECAME PRESIDENT.
Reagan
Reagan
POWER SHIFTED IN WASHINGTON, AND CONGRESS SLASHED NASA'S BUDGET.
THE GALILEO PROJECT WAS ON THE CHOPPING BLOCK.
BUT THE SPACECRAFT IS 90% DONE!

GERMANY WAS NOT HAPPY ABOUT THE CANCELLATION PLANS. THEY HAD ALREADY PUT 40 MILLION DEUTSCH MARKS INTO THE GALILEO MISSION.
FLUSH
40 M
JAMES VAN ALLEN, WHO WAS FAMOUS FOR DISCOVERING THE EARTH'S RADIATION BELTS, LED A LETTER-WRITING CAMPAIGN TO SAVE THE MISSION.
TOGETHER, WE CAN DO THIS.
ASTRONOMERS, SCIENTISTS, AND SPACE FANS FROM AROUND THE WORLD WROTE HUNDREDS OF THOUSANDS OF LETTERS TO THE WHITE HOUSE.
PLEASE.
POR FAVOR.
S'IL VOUS PLAIT.
BITTE.
BUT WILL THE LETTERS SAVE THE MISSION?

THE MANY LETTERS DID THE TRICK, AND IN 1983, THE MISSION WAS SAVED FROM CANCELLATION.

NASA **NOW** HOPED IT WOULD BE ABLE TO LAUNCH GALILEO IN 1986.

DURING THE NEXT THREE YEARS...

GALILEO'S LAUNCH DATE WAS GETTING CLOSER!

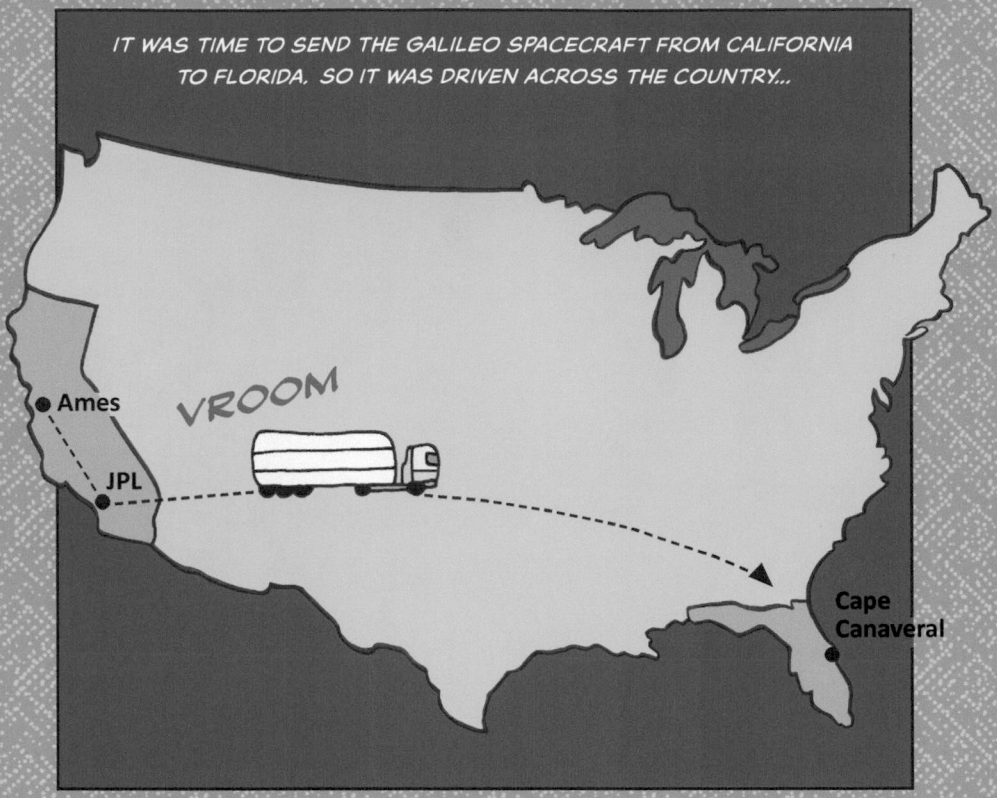
IT WAS TIME TO SEND THE GALILEO SPACECRAFT FROM CALIFORNIA TO FLORIDA. SO IT WAS DRIVEN ACROSS THE COUNTRY...
VROOM
Ames
JPL
Cape Canaveral

...AND BY EARLY 1986, IT WAS IN FLORIDA, WAITING FOR SOME FINAL TESTS BEFORE ITS LAUNCH.
THEN, IN AN INSTANT, EVERYTHING CHANGED.

IT WAS THE WORST DISASTER
THAT NASA HAD EVER HAD.

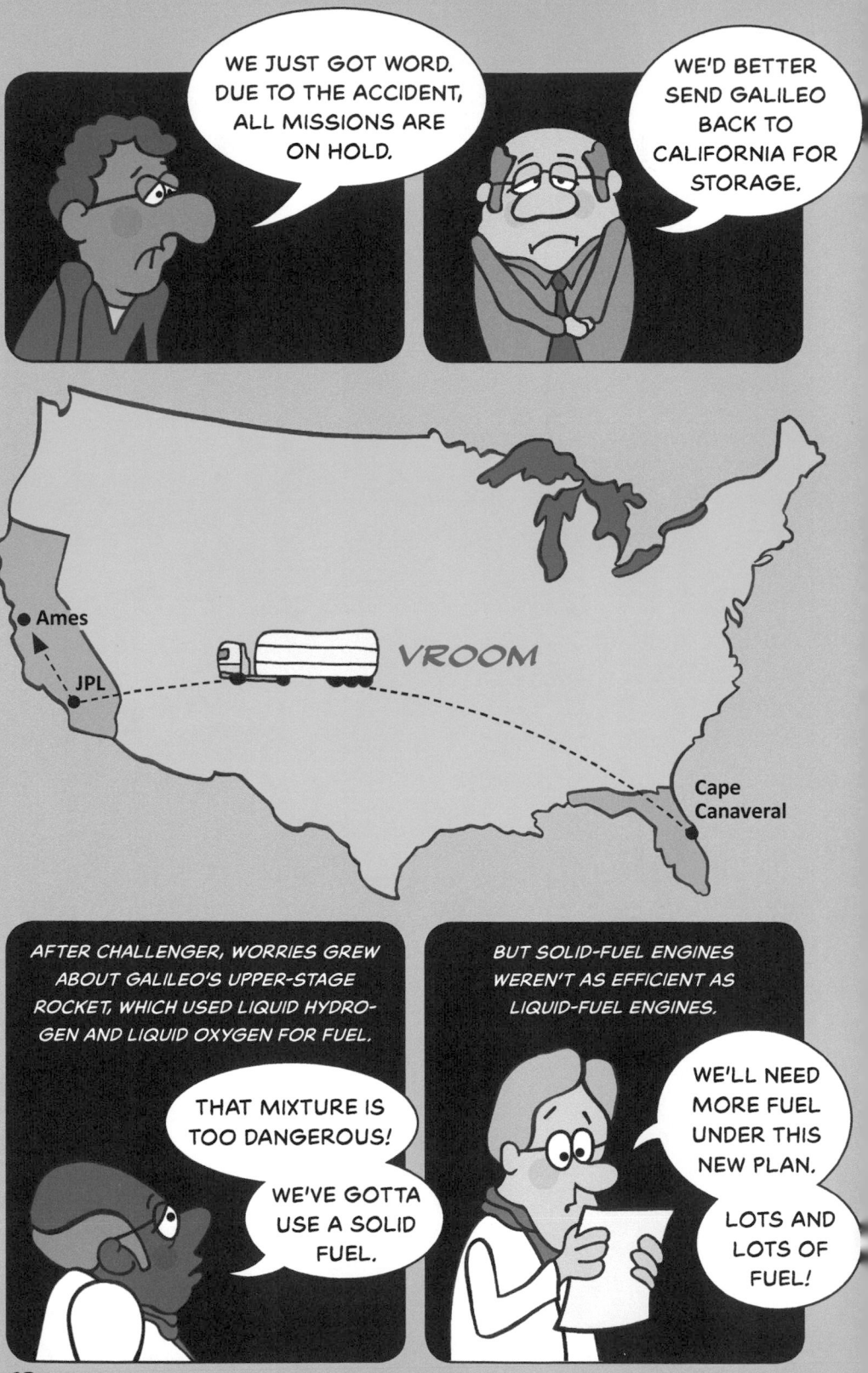
WE JUST GOT WORD. DUE TO THE ACCIDENT, ALL MISSIONS ARE ON HOLD.
WE'D BETTER SEND GALILEO BACK TO CALIFORNIA FOR STORAGE.
Ames
JPL
VROOM
Cape Canaveral
AFTER CHALLENGER, WORRIES GREW ABOUT GALILEO'S UPPER-STAGE ROCKET, WHICH USED LIQUID HYDROGEN AND LIQUID OXYGEN FOR FUEL.
THAT MIXTURE IS TOO DANGEROUS!
WE'VE GOTTA USE A SOLID FUEL.
BUT SOLID-FUEL ENGINES WEREN'T AS EFFICIENT AS LIQUID-FUEL ENGINES.
WE'LL NEED MORE FUEL UNDER THIS NEW PLAN.
LOTS AND LOTS OF FUEL!

IN FACT, IF THE ROCKET TRIED TO CARRY BOTH GALILEO AND THE NEW FUEL, IT WOULD BE TOO HEAVY TO FLY.
23 TONS
FU
FUEL
PLOP
SCIENTISTS WERE DEVASTATED.
THEY DIDN'T SEE ANY WAY TO GET GALILEO OUT TO JUPITER.
? ! ? ! ? ! ?
WHAT?

AFTER ALL THE YEARS SPENT ON THE PROJECT,
IT LOOKED LIKE THE NEW FUEL RULES WOULD END THE MISSION.

AFTER MANY MEETINGS, THEY HATCHED A PLAN.
THEY WOULD USE THE FORCE OF **GRAVITY** TO GET GALILEO TO JUPITER.

SO THEY DECIDED TO GIVE GALILEO **THREE** GRAVITY ASSISTS.
IT WOULD SWING AROUND VENUS, AND THEN TWICE AROUND EARTH.

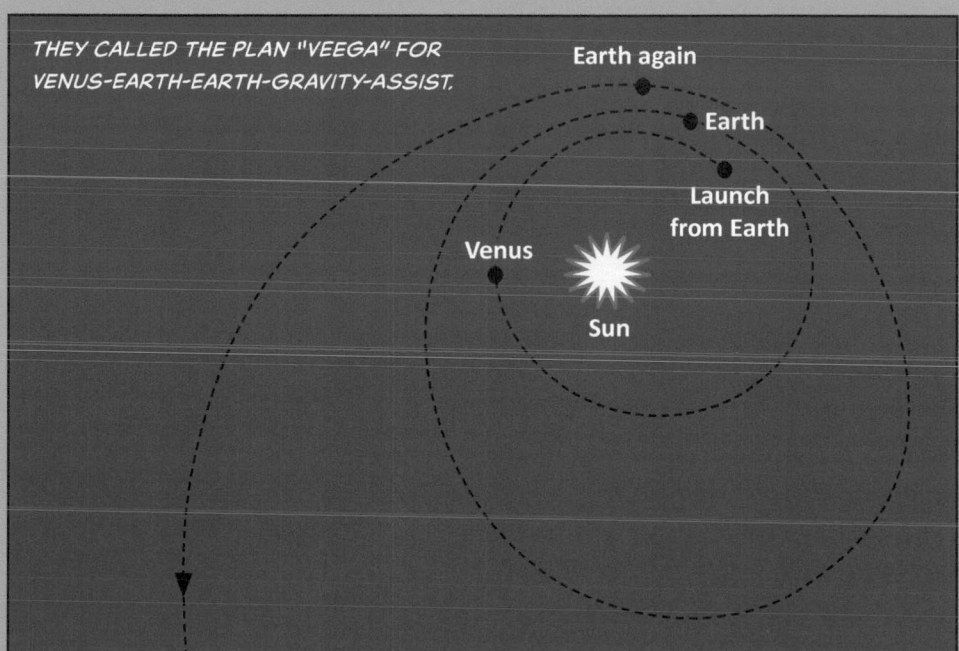

SWINGING AROUND VENUS AND EARTH WILL ADD ***YEARS*** TO THE JOURNEY.
YEP, IT WILL TAKE GALILEO ***SIX YEARS*** TO REACH JUPITER, INSTEAD OF TWO.
HOLY MACKEREL!
AND THERE'S ***ANOTHER*** NEW PROBLEM.
WHAT'S THAT?

SWINGING AROUND VENUS MEANS WE'LL BE HEADING TOWARDS THE SUN.
BUT WE DIDN'T DESIGN GALILEO TO FLY SO CLOSE TO THE SUN.
YIKES! IT'S GOING TO NEED SPECIAL HEAT SHIELDS.
BACK TO THE DRAWING BOARD.
AGAIN.

IN EARLY 1987, GALILEO WAS BACK IN CALIFORNIA -- IN ABOUT A MILLION PIECES.

SCIENTISTS FOUND MANY THINGS THAT WERE OLD AND NEEDED TO BE FIXED.

MEANWHILE IN GERMANY, ENGINEERS HAD STARTED TO WORK ON A SPACECRAFT FOR A DIFFERENT PROJECT.

IT USED THRUSTERS THAT WERE A LOT LIKE THE ONES THEY'D PUT ON GALILEO.

GUESS WHAT?

WHAT?

THE THRUSTERS OVERHEAT AND DESTROY THEMSELVES!

THIS WAS A **HUGE** WORRY BECAUSE GALILEO WOULD NEED GOOD THRUSTERS SO NASA COULD EASE IT ONTO THE RIGHT PATHS FOR ITS JOURNEY.

JPL RECEIVED NEW THRUSTERS FROM GERMANY IN EARLY 1989.

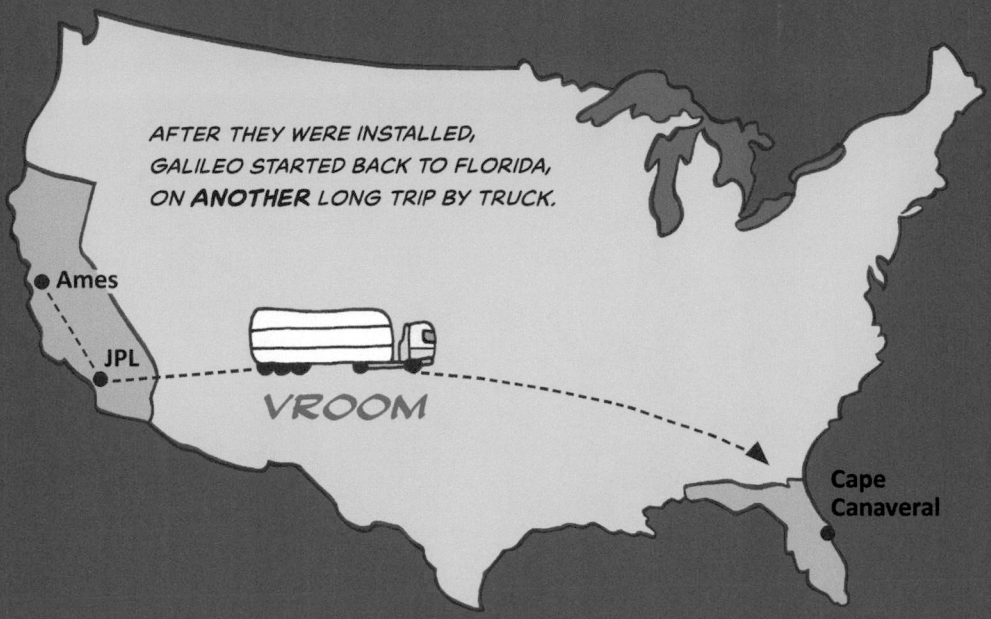

PROTESTORS FIRED AT THE GALILEO SPACECRAFT TODAY.
THEY SAY ITS PLUTONIUM IS A RISK TO THE ENVIRONMENT.
NEWS
SO HOW DID SHOOTING AT IT HELP?
LET'S BACK UP A MINUTE. FOR MUCH OF GALILEO'S JOURNEY TO JUPITER, IT WOULD BE SO FAR AWAY FROM THE SUN THAT IT WOULDN'T BE ABLE TO USE SOLAR POWER.
IT WOULD HAVE TO USE BATTERIES.
THOSE BATTERIES HOLD PELLETS OF PLUTONIUM WHICH WILL DECAY AND PRODUCE ENERGY.
THE ENERGY WILL HELP POWER THE SPACECRAFT.

BY SEPTEMBER 1989, GALILEO HAD REACHED FLORIDA AND WAS NESTLED IN THE CARGO HOLD OF THE SPACE SHUTTLE. BUT PROTESTORS THREATENED TO SIT ON THE SHUTTLE'S LAUNCHPAD, SO NO ONE COULD FIRE ITS ROCKETS.

BUT THE LAUNCH WAS ON HOLD, ON ACCOUNT OF THE PLUTONIUM.

THE PLUTONIUM SCARED PEOPLE.
I CAN CERTAINLY UNDERSTAND.
IN THE PAST DECADE, WE'VE HAD NUCLEAR ACCIDENTS AT THREE MILE ISLAND AND CHERNOBYL.
AND THE CHALLENGER WENT DOWN. WHAT IF GALILEO GOES DOWN TOO? WHAT IF IT CAUSES AN EVEN WORSE NUCLEAR ACCIDENT?
GROUPS THAT WERE NERVOUS ABOUT THE PLUTONIUM WENT TO COURT TO TRY TO STOP THE LAUNCH.
YOUR HONOR, NASA HAS NO EXPERIENCE LAUNCHING NUCLEAR DEVICES FROM THE SPACE SHUTTLE.
ALSO, GALILEO'S PLUTONIUM PELLETS ARE NEARLY TEN YEARS OLD. WHAT IF THEY FRACTURE?

THE FAMOUS ASTRONOMER, CARL SAGAN, STOOD UP FOR GALILEO AGAIN. HE BELIEVED MUCH GOOD COULD COME FROM THE MISSION, AND THE CHANCE OF A PLUTONIUM ACCIDENT WAS SMALL. IN A NEWSPAPER ARTICLE, HE WROTE...

"There is nothing absurd about either side of this argument. But considering the possibility that many more lives might be saved because of Galileo's findings, my personal vote is to launch."

HOWEVER, ON OCTOBER 16TH, THE DAY BEFORE THE LAUNCH WAS SUPPOSED TO TAKE PLACE, NASA EMPLOYEES ARRIVED AT THEIR OFFICES TO A HUGE SURPRISE.

ALL THEIR COMPUTERS HAD BEEN HACKED!

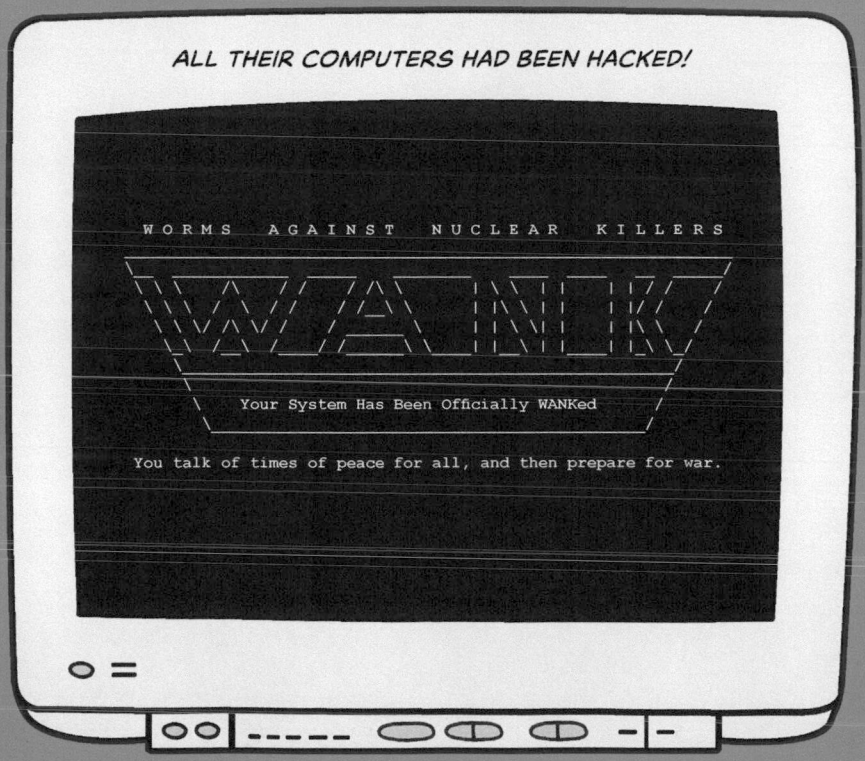

IT WAS A COMPUTER WORM, AND IT SEEMED TO BE DELETING ALL THEIR FILES. HAD NASA LOST CONTROL OF ITS COMPUTERS?

THE NEXT DAY, AS THE WORM CONTINUED TO SPREAD, NASA POSTPONED GALILEO'S LAUNCH.

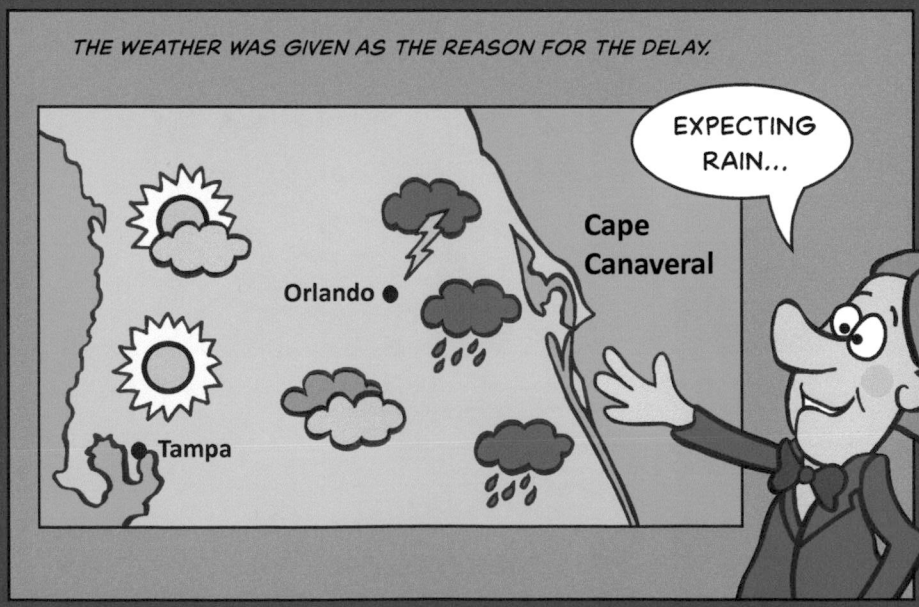

HOURS AFTER THE LAUNCH WAS CANCELLED, NASA AND DOE CAME UP WITH ANTI-WORM PROGRAMS.

HE PRESSED THE "SEND" KEY AND LEFT THE BUILDING.

SIXTY-THREE PEOPLE DIED. OVER 3,500 WERE INJURED. THE QUAKE'S DESTRUCTION COST BILLIONS.

IT STALLED GALILEO BECAUSE TWO FLIGHT CENTERS IN CALIFORNIA (AMES AND ONIZUKA) WERE DAMAGED.

HOWEVER, BY THE NEXT MORNING, THE TWO FLIGHT CENTERS WERE UP AND RUNNING AGAIN.

AND SO, AFTER YEARS OF TECHNICAL AND POLITICAL PROBLEMS, PLUS SOME FINAL DAYS OF LEGAL BATTLES, HACKERS, AND EVEN A GIGANTIC EARTHQUAKE, GALILEO FINALLY LAUNCHED.

ON OCTOBER 18, 1989, GALILEO LEFT EARTH ON THE SPACE SHUTTLE.

THE GALILEO SPACECRAFT WEIGHED TWO AND A HALF TONS, AND IT SAT IN THE SHUTTLE'S CARGO HOLD, WAITING FOR THE CREW TO FREE IT.

SINCE THERE WERE NO ASTRONAUTS ABOARD THE GALILEO SPACECRAFT, NASA WATCHED AND MANAGED EVERYTHING FROM EARTH.

IT TOOK FOUR MONTHS FOR GALILEO TO REACH VENUS, THE FIRST POINT ON ITS VEEGA PATH.

AFTER GALILEO PASSED VENUS, IT STARTED BACK TOWARDS EARTH.

EIGHT MONTHS LATER, IN LATE 1990, IT FLEW BY EARTH AND PICKED UP **MORE** MOMENTUM.

THIS ROBBED EARTH OF A TINY BIT OF ENERGY, WHICH MEANS THAT IN A BILLION YEARS, EARTH WILL BE FIVE INCHES BEHIND, IN ITS ORBIT AROUND THE SUN.

AS GALILEO PASSED EARTH, IT RAN TESTS ON OUR ATMOSPHERE. IT ALSO MAPPED THE SOUTH POLE-AITKEN BASIN ON THE FAR SIDE OF OUR MOON. IT'S ONE OF THE BIGGEST CRATERS IN OUR SOLAR SYSTEM.

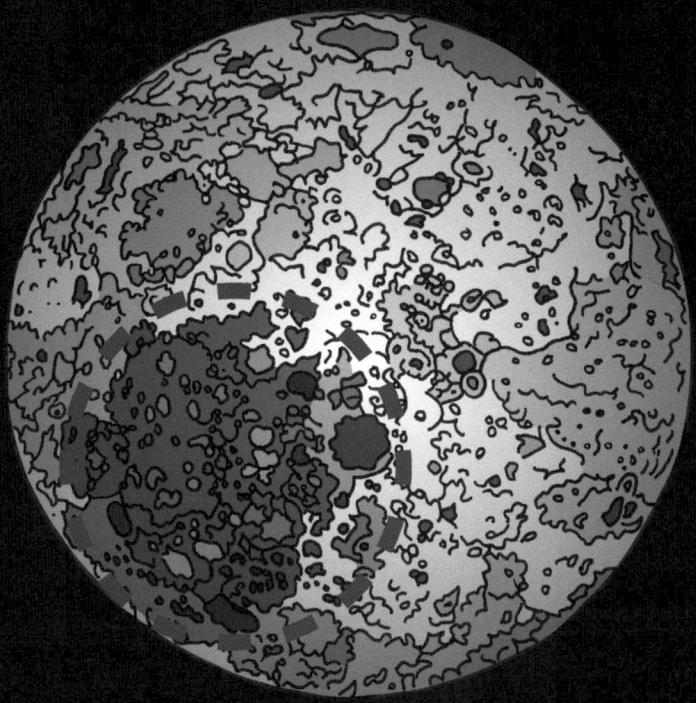

THE CRATER IS 1,600 MILES ACROSS. THAT'S NEARLY SIX GRAND CANYONS!

GALILEO STILL NEEDED TO PASS EARTH A SECOND TIME, SO IT KEPT FLYING.

IT HAD BEEN IN SPACE FOR A YEAR AND A HALF, AND DURING ALL THAT TIME, ITS BEST ANTENNA HAD BEEN FOLDED UP UNDER A HEAT SHIELD TO PROTECT IT FROM THE SUN.

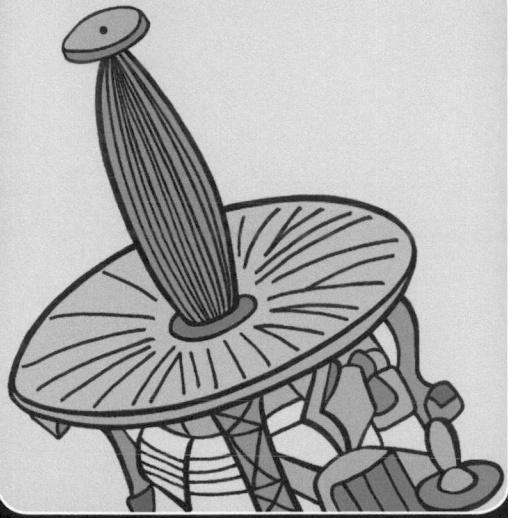

NOW GALILEO WAS ENTERING THE ASTEROID BELT, WHERE THINGS WERE SUPPOSED TO GET REALLY INTERESTING.

IT WAS TIME TO USE THE ANTENNA!

O IN APRIL
71, ONE OF
HE FLIGHT
TROLLERS
T GALILEO
SIGNAL TO
OPEN THE
ANTENNA.

NASA WAS COMPLETELY SHOCKED AND CONFUSED! THEY SENT MORE SIGNALS TO GALILEO, TO TEST IT.

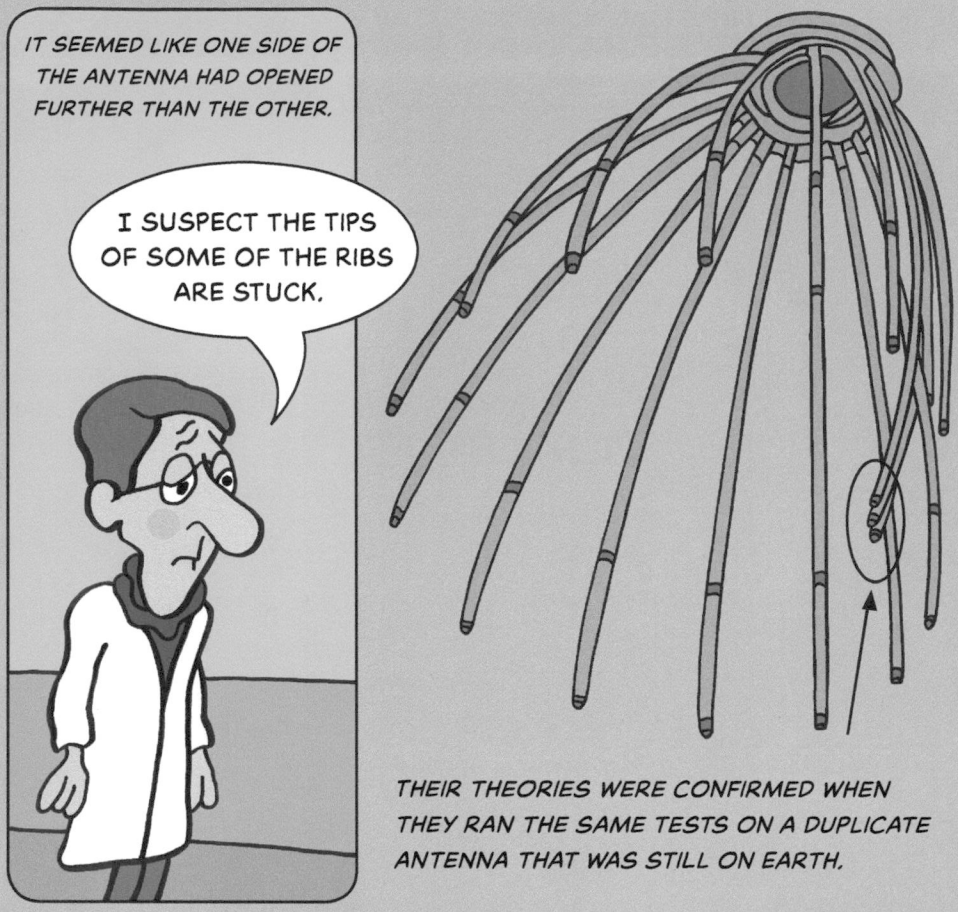

THE SCIENTISTS TRIED MANY WAYS TO FREE THE ANTENNA'S RIBS.
LET'S POINT GALILEO TOWARDS THE SUN, AND THEN AWAY.
MAYBE THAT WILL CAUSE EXPANSIONS AND CONTRACTIONS THAT WILL LOOSEN THE RIBS.
THAT DIDN'T WORK.
LET'S SWITCH THE MOTOR ON AND OFF MANY TIMES. MAYBE THAT WILL SHAKE THE RIBS FREE.
THAT DIDN'T WORK EITHER.
LET'S SPIN THE SPACECRAFT TO APPLY CENTRIFUGAL FORCE TO THE RIBS.
NOR DID THAT HELP.
NO KIDDING!

I BET SOME OIL EVAPORATED DURING THE ANTENNA'S STORAGE.
OR DURING THOSE LONG TRIPS ACROSS COUNTRY.
OR MAYBE THE OIL WORE AWAY! AFTER ALL, THE RIBS HAVE BEEN CONSTANTLY RUBBING AGAINST THE MAST.
I WISH I COULD JUST GO OUT THERE WITH AN OIL CAN.
glug
SINCE IT WASN'T CLEAR HOW TO OPEN THE FAST ANTENNA, NASA BEGAN TO THINK ABOUT SOME SLOW ANTENNAS THAT WERE ALSO ON GALILEO.

WE WERE EXPECTING THE FAST ANTENNA TO SEND BACK 134,000 BITS OF DATA PER SECOND.
THE SLOW ANTENNAS CAN ONLY SEND 10 BITS PER SECOND.
AT 10 BITS PER SECOND, IT WOULD TAKE FOUR WEEKS TO TRANSMIT A SINGLE IMAGE.
THAT WOULD BE A DISASTER! GALILEO IS SUPPOSED TO SEND BACK TENS OF THOUSANDS OF IMAGES.
SLICE
BUT THE ONLY ANTENNAS THAT WERE WORKING WERE THE SLOW ONES.
SAD BUT TRUE.

GALILEO KEPT GOING. IN OCTOBER 1991, IT BECAME THE FIRST SPACECRAFT TO FLY CLOSE TO AN ASTEROID.
THIS IS LIKE COLUMBUS LANDING IN THE NEW WORLD.
WE'RE GETTING AN AMAZING LOOK AT A NEW TYPE OF OBJECT.
FASCINATING!
A RUSSIAN ASTRONOMER HAD DISCOVERED THIS ASTEROID FROM EARTH, BACK IN 1916.
I NAMED IT "GASPRA" AFTER MY FAVORITE PLACE ON THE BLACK SEA.
Grigory Neujmin
IT WAS HARD TO GET DATA ABOUT GASPRA BACK TO EARTH BECAUSE THE FAST ANTENNA WAS STILL CLOSED.

HOWEVER, BY USING THE SLOW ANTENNAS, AND CAMERAS, AND OTHER INSTRUMENTS, SCIENTISTS WERE ABLE TO LEARN QUITE A BIT.

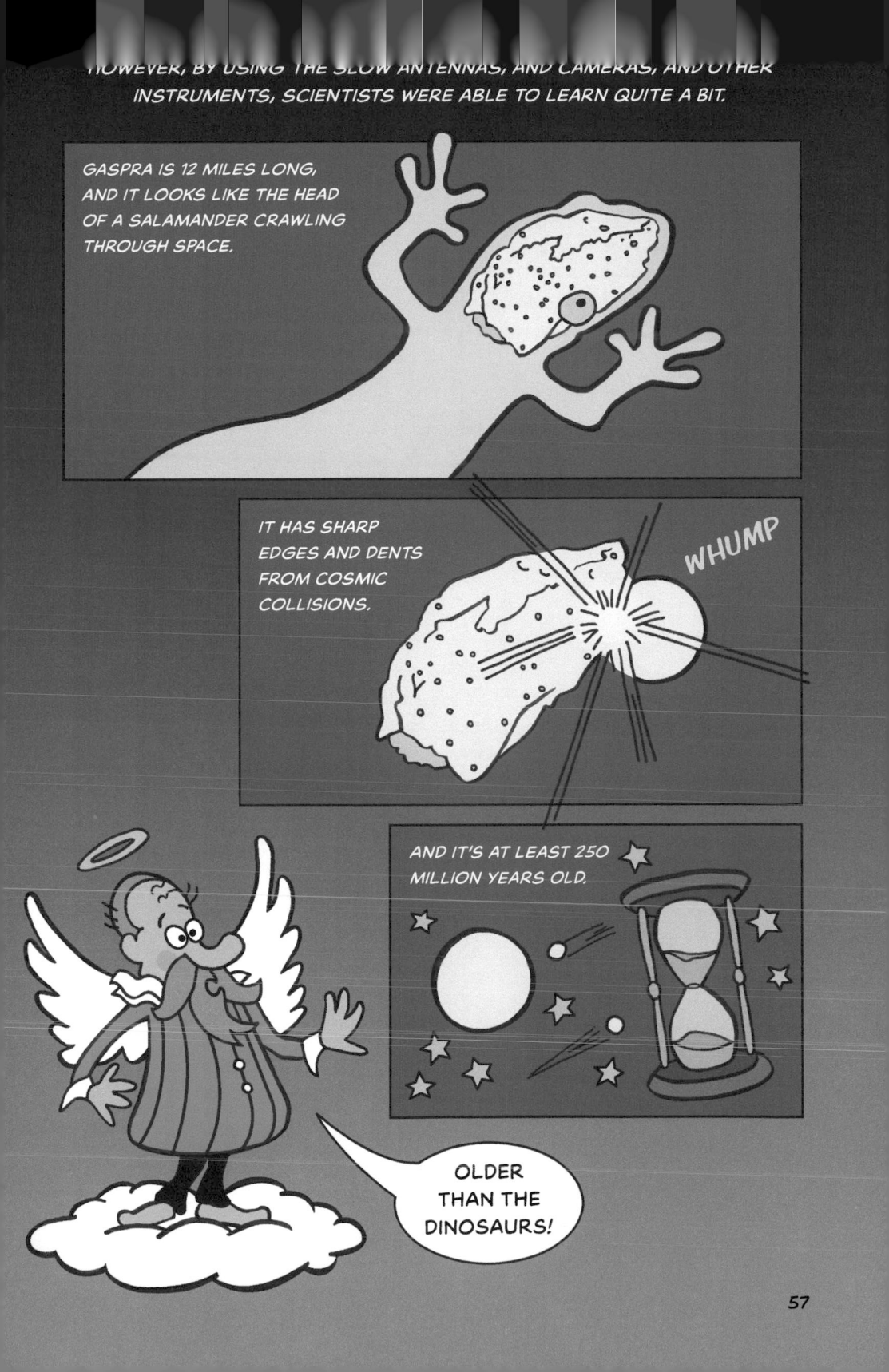

AFTER GALILEO PASSED GASPRA, IT HEADED BACK TO EARTH FOR THE SECOND TIME.
THAT WAS IN 1992, WHEN THE FIRST TEXT MESSAGE WAS SENT...
MERRY CHRISTMAS
ORBITEL
MENU
C
F
MR
1 ABC
2 DEF
3 GHI
...AND DOUGLAS ADAMS FINISHED HIS FIVE-BOOK TRILOGY, THE HITCHHIKER'S GUIDE TO THE GALAXY ...
"Space is big. Really big. You just won't believe how vastly, hugely, mind-boggingly big it is."
...AND POPE JOHN PAUL II GAVE GALILEO AN APOLOGY, 350 YEARS AFTER THE ASTRONOMER HAD DIED.
WELL, NOW I CAN SLEEP AT NIGHT.

THE EARTH FLY-BYS GAVE SCIENTISTS A BETTER UNDERSTANDING OF...
...OUR MESOPHERE, THE COLDEST PART OF OUR ATMOSPHERE...
exosphere
thermosphere
mesosphere
stratosphere
troposphere
Earth
...AND OUR OZONE HOLE OVER ANTARCTICA...
...AND OUR NORTHERN LIGHTS.
Earth
Mars
Asteroid Belt
Jupiter
THIS SECOND TRIP BY EARTH ALSO HELPED GALILEO GATHER THE FINAL MOMENTUM FOR ITS JOURNEY TO JUPITER.

IN 1993, GALILEO ENTERED THE ASTEROID BELT FOR THE SECOND TIME. THIS TIME, IT FLEW CLOSE TO **ANOTHER** ASTEROID.

WHEN IDA'S PHOTO REACHED EARTH, IT CREATED LOADS OF EXCITEMENT BECAUSE IDA HAD A MOON!

UNTIL THEN, IT HADN'T BEEN CLEAR THAT ASTEROIDS COULD EVEN **HAVE** MOONS.

DATA FROM IDA AND ITS MOON TOOK A LONG TIME TO REACH EARTH BECAUSE THE FAST ANTENNA STILL WASN'T WORKING.

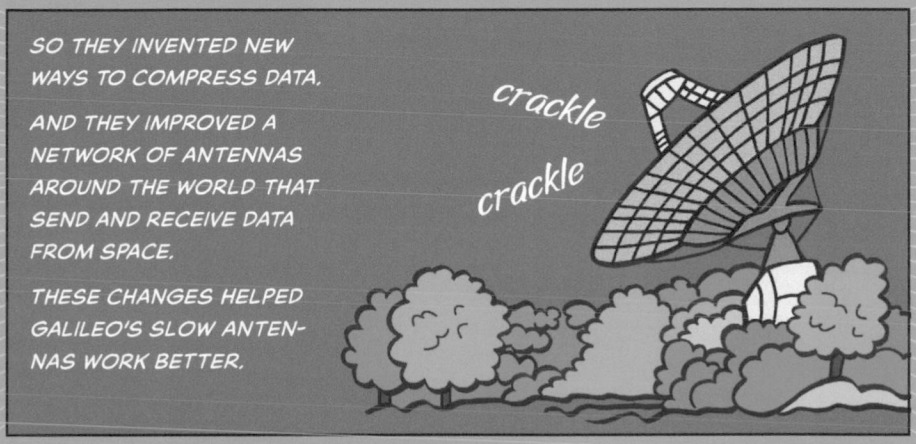

AS GALILEO FLEW THROUGH THE ASTEROID BELT, LIFE CONTINUED ON EARTH.

...AND THE WORLD WAS FASCINATED WITH A COMET.

ONE SPRING NIGHT IN 1993, THREE ASTRONOMERS WERE SEARCHING THE SKY. THEIR NAMES WERE CAROLYN SHOEMAKER, EUGENE SHOEMAKER, AND DAVID LEVY.

IT WAS THE STRANGEST COMET THEY HAD EVER SEEN. TORN APART BY JUPITER'S GRAVITY, ITS PIECES WERE TRAVELING TOGETHER LIKE A STRING OF PEARLS.
THE FRAGMENTS WERE NAMED SHOEMAKER-LEVY 9.
AND SOON, SCIENTISTS REALIZED THAT THE FRAGMENTS WERE ON A COLLISION COURSE WITH JUPITER! NEVER BEFORE HAD HUMANS KNOWN ABOUT A COLLISION BETWEEN HEAVENLY BODIES BEFORE IT WAS GOING TO HAPPEN.
THE UPCOMING COLLISION CREATED WORLDWIDE EXCITEMENT...
...UNTIL WE REALIZED THE FRAGMENTS WOULD CRASH INTO THE FAR SIDE OF JUPITER.
COMPLETELY OUT OF THE EARTH'S SIGHT.
BUT THEN PEOPLE REALIZED THERE WAS STILL A WAY TO WATCH THE COMING COLLISION.
BY THEN, GALILEO SHOULD BE IN SIGHT OF JUPITER.

IN THE SUMMER OF 1994, THE COMET'S FRAGMENTS SMASHED INTO JUPITER.

JUST **ONE** OF THE CRASHES WAS 600 TIMES AS STRONG AS ALL THE NUCLEAR BOMBS ON EARTH COMBINED.

BOOM!

BOOM!

KABLOOM!

WHEREVER THE FRAGMENTS HIT JUPITER, DARK SCARS REMAINED FOR MONTHS.

SOME OF THE SCARS WERE TWO TO THREE TIMES THE SIZE OF EARTH.

FEW MONTHS LATER, GALILEO FINALLY REACHED JUPITER! IT HAD BEEN 5
RS SINCE IT HAD LEFT EARTH, AND 20 YEARS SINCE THE PROJECT HAD BEG

IT WEIGHED 750 POUNDS, AND IT WAS THE FIRST PROBE TO
ENTER THE ATMOSPHERE OF ONE OF THE OUTER PLANETS

FOR YEARS, THE PROBE HAD BEEN SITTING IN FRONT OF AN ENGINE, SO NONE OF THE FLIGHT CONTROLLERS HAD BEEN ALLOWED TO START UP THAT ENGINE.

DID THE VALVE CLOSE? IF IT DIDN'T, TWO FUELS MIGHT BE MIXING TOGETHER,
CAUSING UNDESIRABLE CHEMICAL REACTIONS.
WHAT YOU'RE REALLY SAYING IS THAT THE ORBITER COULD BLOW ITSELF TO SMITHEREENS.
KABOOM?
LUCKILY, THEY WERE ABLE TO FIX THE PROBLEM. THE DANGER PASSED, THE ENGINE STARTED, AND GALILEO SETTLED INTO JUPITER'S ORBIT.

A FEW MONTHS LATER, **ANOTHER** PROBLEM POPPED UP.

SO ONE MORNING, MISSION CONTROL ON EARTH SENT A COMMAND TO GALILEO'S TAPE RECORDER:

> REWIND TO STORED PHOTOS OF JUPITER

BUT THE TAPE RECORDER ONLY SPUN ITS WHEELS.

I KNOW THE FEELING.

NASA WAS STUNNED.
WHY DID THE TAPE RECORDER FAIL?
MUCH LATER, THEY WERE HORRIFIED TO LEARN THAT THE PRESSURE ROLLER ON THE TAPE RECORDER WAS STILL SPINNING.
FOR THE LAST 15 HOURS, THE ROLLER HAS WORN AGAINST THE SAME SPOT ON THE TAPE!
BY SOME MIRACLE, THE TAPE HASN'T WORN THROUGH AND SNAPPED IN TWO.
WITHOUT THE TAPE RECORDER, THEY WOULDN'T BE ABLE TO STORE DATA.
LUCKILY, THINGS LOOKED BETTER IN A FEW DAYS. TESTS SHOWED THAT IF THE TAPE RECORDER WAS USED AT A SLOW SPEED, IT MIGHT STILL WORK.
WHAT GOOD NEWS!
NOW WE HAVE TO MAKE SOME TOUGH DECISIONS.
SINCE THE PROBE HAD BEEN A KEY PART OF THE MISSION FROM THE VERY BEGINNING, NASA WAS DETERMINED TO GET ITS DATA BACK TO EARTH.
THEY DECIDED TO GO EASY ON THE TAPE RECORDER UNTIL THE PROBE'S PART OF THE MISSION WAS DONE, BUT THAT MEANT THEY WOULDN'T BE ABLE TO RETRIEVE EARLY OBSERVATIONS OF JUPITER OR ITS MOONS.

MEANWHILE, THROUGH THE SUMMER AND AUTUMN OF 1995, THE PROBE HAD BEEN FALLING THROUGH JUPITER'S ATMOSPHERE.

AS THE SCIENTISTS WAITED FOR THE MONTHS TO PASS, THEY WORRIED.

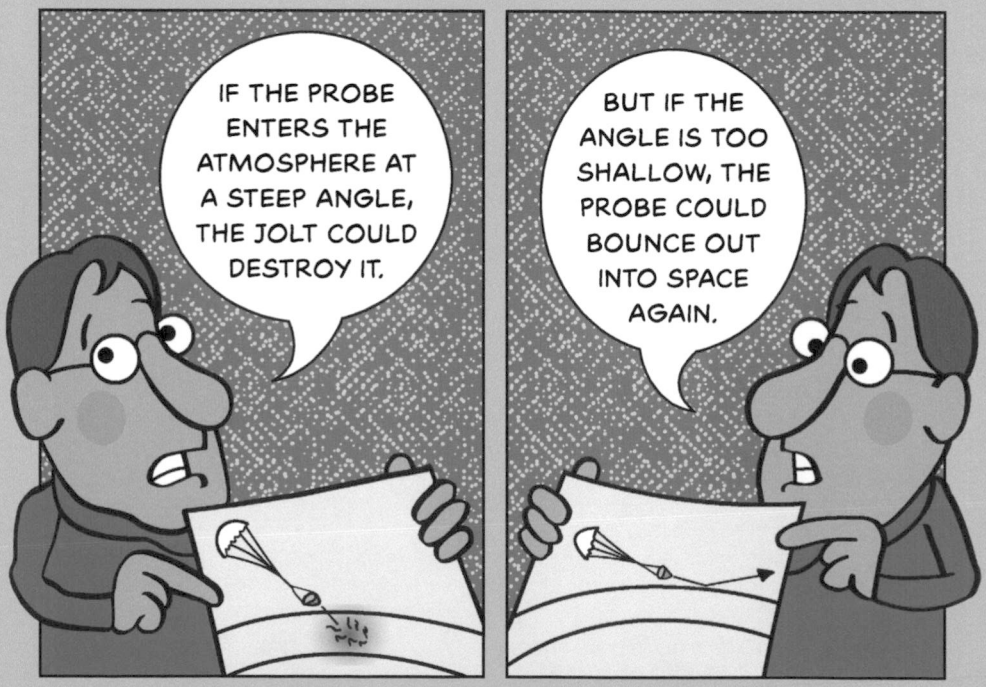

AND EVEN IF THE PROBE ENTERED PERFECTLY, IT WOULD STILL FACE TEMPERATURES THAT WERE TWICE AS HOT AS THE SURFACE OF THE SUN.

PHEW!

FINALLY, THE DAY ARRIVED WHEN THE PROBE WAS SUPPOSED TO WAKE UP.

BUT THEY GREW MORE AND MORE ANXIOUS BECAUSE NO SIGNAL ARRIVED.

THERE WAS ONLY SILENCE.

TENSELY, THEY WAITED — AND WONDERED.

FINALLY, A SIGNAL ARRIVED! IT SHOWED THAT THE PROBE HAD BEEN SENDING DATA TO THE ORBITER.

AS THE PROBE FELL, IT COLLECTED DATA ABOUT...

THAT WAS EXACTLY HOW NASA HAD EXPECTED THINGS TO TURN OUT.

IN THE END, THE PROBE SIMPLY MELTED.

THE GALILEO TEAM TOOK A MOMENT TO REFLECT ON THE MISSION SO FAR.

AFTER THE DATA FROM THE PROBE WAS RECEIVED, NASA SET THE ORBITER ON A PATH TO FLY FROM MOON TO MOON.
ITS PRIMARY MISSION HAD FINALLY BEGUN.
Jupiter
Io
Europa
Ganymede
Callisto
IT WILL ORBIT JUPITER AND HAVE CLOSE ENCOUNTERS WITH ITS MAJOR MOONS!

DURING THE PRIMARY MISSION, THE ORBITER SENT SOME FASCINATING DATA BACK TO EARTH.

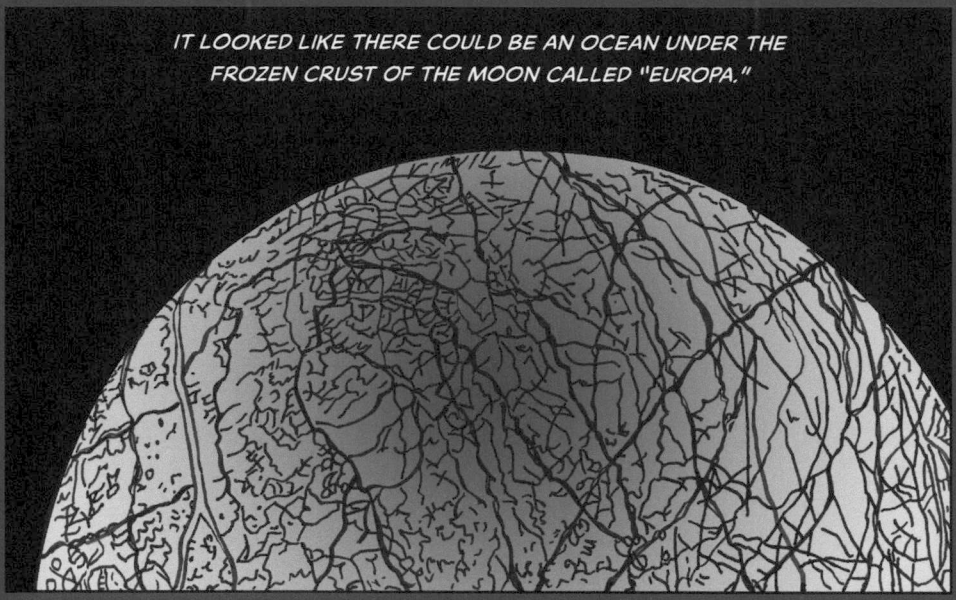

THAT'S AN ENVIRONMENT WHERE LIFE COULD EXIST.

AND **THAT** CERTAINLY CAUGHT THE WORLD'S ATTENTION!

IT WAS POSSIBLE.

THE ORBITER'S PRIMARY MISSION WAS SUPPOSED TO WIND DOWN IN 1997, BUT WHEN THAT TIME CAME, IT WAS WORKING FINE, AND IT STILL HAD FUEL.

SO NASA EXTENDED THE MISSION FOR TWO MORE YEARS TO LOOK VERY CLOSELY AT THE MOONS EUROPA AND IO.

IO HAS THE MOST POWERFUL VOLCANO IN OUR SOLAR SYSTEM. IT'S CALLED "LOKI," AND IT CREATES MORE HEAT THAN ALL THE VOLCANOES ON EARTH COMBINED.

WHEN 1999 CAME, THE MISSION WAS SUPPOSED TO END.
BUT THE ORBITER WAS STILL WORKING!

SO THE MISSION WAS EXTENDED AGAIN, UNTIL 2001.

GALILEO COLLECTED DATA AS IT FLEW CLOSE TO EUROPA, IO, AND CALLISTO.

WHEN 2001 CAME, THE MISSION WAS SUPPOSED TO END.

SO THE MISSION WAS EXTENDED AGAIN, UNTIL 2003.

THIS TIME, GALILEO STUDIED THE MOONS IO, GANYMEDE, AND AMALTHEA.

IN ALL, DURING THE PRIMARY AND EXTENDED MISSIONS, GALILEO HAD 35 ENCOUNTERS WITH JUPITER'S MOONS.

HERE ARE JUST A FEW OF GALILEO'S FINDINGS.
It measured chemicals that offered clues to Jupiter's evolution.
9% helium
90% hydrogen
1% methane, water vapor, phosphorus, ammonia, carbon, and sulfur
It closely observed the Great Red Spot.
It discovered a magnetosphere around Ganymede. Never before had one been found around a moon.
Ganymede
It mapped Jupiter's magnetosphere, which is 100 times as large as the sun!
Jupiter
It studied the causes and effects of volcanoes on Io.
It found clues for oceans beneath the frozen crusts of Europa, Ganymede, and Callisto.
Even years later, we're still making discoveries from the mission.
GALILEO'S DATA SUGGESTS GEYSERS ERUPT ON EUROPA!

DURING THE EXTENDED MISSIONS, SCIENTISTS TALKED ABOUT HOW TO PROTECT THEIR DISCOVERIES WHILE THEY WRAPPED UP THE ORBITER'S JOURNEY.

IF IT FELL OUT OF ORBIT, THERE WAS A TINY CHANCE IT COULD RETURN TO EARTH.

EVERYONE AGREED THAT THEY SHOULDN'T LET THE ORBITER CRASH INTO EUROPA OR ANY OF THE OTHER MOONS THAT MIGHT CONTAIN LIFE.

THAT MEANT ITS EARTH MICROBES COULD OVERRUN INDIGENOUS MICROBES, IF THERE WAS ANY POSSIBILITY OF LIFE ON THOSE MOONS.

NASA DECIDED THAT IT WOULD BE BEST TO CRASH THE ORBITER INTO JUPITER, WHICH DIDN'T HAVE ANY OF THE CONDITIONS THAT SUPPORT LIFE.

AND BY 2003, THAT PLAN WAS BECOMING NECESSARY...

AND SO THEY SET THE ORBITER ON A COLLISION COURSE WITH JUPITER.

IN THE AUTUMN OF 2003, HUNDREDS OF SCIENTISTS, ENGINEERS, AND THEIR FAMILIES GATHERED AT JPL.
ALTHOUGH THEY COULDN'T SEE GALILEO, THEY COULD IMAGINE IT. TOGETHER, THEY COUNTED DOWN THE FINAL SECONDS OF ITS JOURNEY.
TEN, NINE, EIGHT...
SEVEN, SIX, FIVE, FOUR...
THREE, TWO, ONE...
BYE!

IN THE END, DUE TO JUPITER'S GRAVITY, GALILEO FELL AT 108,000 MILES PER HOUR. THAT'S LIKE SPEEDING FROM LOS ANGELES TO NEW YORK CITY IN 82 SECONDS.
WHOOSH
GALILEO CRASHED INTO JUPITER ON SEPTEMBER 21, 2003.
ITS LAST MESSAGE REACHED EARTH AFTER THE SPACECRAFT HAD ALREADY BEEN DESTROYED.
AT THE SPEED OF LIGHT, THE MESSAGE TOOK AN HOUR TO CROSS HALF A BILLION MILES OF SPACE, AND IT HELD GALILEO'S LAST SCIENTIFIC MEASUREMENTS.

THE GALILEO MISSION TURNED OUT TO BE ONE OF NASA'S HARDEST PROJECTS.

FOR A QUARTER OF A CENTURY, THE PEOPLE ON THE MISSION USED THEIR IMAGINATIONS TO OVERCOME TOUGH PROBLEMS, SOME OF WHICH CAME UP WHEN THE SPACECRAFT WAS MILLIONS OF MILES AWAY.

GALILEO RECOVERED OVER AND OVER AGAIN.

WITH BRILLIANT BREAKTHROUGHS AND UNEXPECTED DISCOVERIES, IT WAS A SPECTACULAR MISSION!

NOW THAT YOU'VE READ THIS STORY, WHY DO **YOU** THINK THE GALILEO TEAM KEPT GOING?

HAVE YOU EVER KEPT GOING, EVEN THOUGH IT WAS TOUGH?

HOW DO YOU USE **YOUR** IMAGINATION TO SOLVE PROBLEMS?

WHAT SPACE MISSION WOULD BE MOST EXCITING TO **YOU**?

DO YOU EVER DREAM OF UNKNOWN WORLDS?

CAN YOU SEE YOURSELF SETTING SAIL FOR THE PLANETS?

WHEN YOU LOOK UP AT THE STARS, WHAT DO **YOU** IMAGINE?

ONE LAST THING....
WHY DID THE CHICKEN CROSS THE SOLAR SYSTEM?
BYE!
TO BOLDLY GO WHERE NO CHICKEN HAS GONE BEFORE.

BIBLIOGRAPHY

CASANI, JOHN (GALILEO PROJECT MANAGER), INTERVIEW BY JOHN KRIGE, MAY 18, 2009, PASADENA, CALIFORNIA.

CRAWFORD, J. CRAIG. "GROUP SAYS GALILEO FUEL OLD, DANGEROUS." *ORLANDO SENTINEL*, OCTOBER 5, 1989.

DAWSON, VIRGINIA P., AND MARK D. BOWLES. *TAMING LIQUID HYDROGEN: THE CENTAUR UPPER STAGE ROCKET 1958-2002.* WASHINGTON, DC: NATIONAL AERONAUTICS AND SPACE ADMINISTRATION, OFFICE OF EXTERNAL RELATIONS, 2007.

FISCHER, DANIEL. *MISSION JUPITER: THE SPECTACULAR JOURNEY OF THE GALILEO SPACECRAFT.* NEW YORK: COPERNICUS BOOKS, 2001.

GALILEO TO JUPITER: PROBING THE PLANET AND MAPPING ITS MOONS. PASADENA, CALIFORNIA: NATIONAL AERONAUTICS AND SPACE ADMINISTRATION, CALIFORNIA INSTITUE OF TECHNOLOGY, JET PROPULSION LABORATORY, 1979.

HANLON, MICHAEL. *THE WORLDS OF GALILEO: THE INSIDE STORY OF NASA'S MISSION TO JUPITER.* LONDON: CONSTABLE PUBLISHERS, 2001.

HARLAND, DAVID M. *JUPITER ODYSSEY: THE STORY OF NASA'S GALILEO MISSION.* CHICHESTER, UK: SPRINGER-PRAXIS BOOKS, 2000.

HARLAND, DAVID M., AND RALPH D. LORENZ. *SPACE SYSTEM FAILURES: DISASTERS AND RESCUES OF SATELLITES, ROCKETS AND SPACE PROBES.* CHICHESTER, UK: SPRINGER-PRAXIS BOOKS IN ASTRONOMY AND SPACE SCIENCES, 2005.

LOGSDON, JOHN M. "THE SURVIVAL CRISIS OF THE US SOLAR SYSTEM EXPLORATION PROGRAM IN THE 1980S." IN *EXPLORING THE SOLAR*

SYSTEM: THE HISTORY AND SCIENCE OF PLANETARY EXPLORATION., EDITED BY ROGER D. LAUNIUS. NEW YORK: PALGRAVE MACMILLAN, 2013.

MELTZER, MICHAEL. *MISSION TO JUPITER: A HISTORY OF THE GALILEO PROJECT.* WASHINGTON, DC: NATIONAL AERONAUTICS AND SPACE ADMINISTRATION, NASA HISTORY DIVISION, 2007.

MESTEL, ROSIE. "CAROLYN SHOEMAKER AND 'HER COMET.'" *NEW SCIENTIST* 143 (JULY 9, 1994): 23.

MOORE, ARDEN. "GALILEO FINALLY HEADS TO JUPITER." *SOUTH FLORIDA SUN SENTINEL*, OCTOBER 19, 1989.

NILSEN, ERIK N., AND P.A. "TRISHA" JANSMA. "GALILEO'S ROCKY ROAD TO JUPITER." *ASK MAGAZINE*, NO. 42 (SPRING 2011).

SAGAN, CARL. "BENEFIT OUTWEIGHS RISK: LAUNCH GALILEO CRAFT." *USA TODAY*, OCTOBER 10, 1989.

SPACE EXPLORATION: NASA'S DEEP SPACE MISSIONS ARE EXPERIENCING LONG DELAYS; BRIEFING REPORT TO THE CHAIRMAN, SUBCOMMITTEE ON SCIENCE, TECHNOLOGY, AND SPACE, COMMITTEE ON COMMERCE, SCIENCE, AND TRANSPORTATION, U.S. SENATE. WASHINGTON, DC: GENERAL ACCOUNTING OFFICE, 1988.

WIKIPEDIA, THE FREE ENCYCLOPEDIA, S.V. "COMET SHOEMAKER-LEVY 9," (ACCESSED MARCH 12, 2020), HTTPS://EN.WIKIPEDIA.ORG/WIKI/COMET_SHOEMAKER%E2%80%93LEVY_9

WIKIPEDIA, THE FREE ENCYCLOPEDIA, S.V. "STS-34," (ACCESSED MARCH 12, 2020), HTTPS://EN.WIKIPEDIA.ORG/WIKI/STS-34

WIKIPEDIA, THE FREE ENCYCLOPEDIA, S.V. "WANK (COMPUTER WORM)," (ACCESSED MARCH 12, 2020), HTTPS://EN.WIKIPEDIA.ORG/WIKI/WANK_(COMPUTER_WORM)

ACKNOWLEDGEMENTS

HOLLY (THOMASON) TRECHTER HAD THE EXCITING OPPORTUNITY TO DO AN INTERNSHIP AT THE NASA AMES HISTORY ARCHIVES. WITH THE INDISPENSABLE HELP OF HER SUPERVISOR, APRIL GAGE, SHE ARCHIVED THE PAPERS OF JOHN D. MIHALOV (HTTPS://HISTORY.ARC.NASA.GOV/HIST_PDFS/GUIDES/PP0522JM_MIHALOV.PDF).

MR. MIHALOV WAS A CO-INVESTIGATOR ON THE GALILEO PROJECT, AND AS HOLLY READ HIS PAPERS, SHE BECAME FASCINATED WITH THE GALILEO MISSION. SHE WANTED TO SHARE ITS STORY WITH KIDS, SO SHE WORKED WITH HER SISTER, JANE DONOVAN, TO CREATE THIS BOOK.

HOLLY AND JANE ARE THANKFUL THAT THEY COULD USE NASA'S PHOTO ARCHIVES. THEY ARE ALSO INDEBTED TO THE AMAZING APRIL GAGE, WHO ARCHIVES DOCUMENTS AND ARTIFACTS FROM MANY NASA MISSIONS. HER GENEROUS WELCOME AND ENCOURAGEMENT MADE THIS BOOK POSSIBLE.

THE AUTHORS ARE ALSO GRATEFUL TO R. KEVIN OBERMAN, WHO WAS THE DEPARTMENT OF ENERGY ENGINEER WHO RELEASED THE ANTI-WORM FIX DURING THE LOMA PRIETA EARTHQUAKE. MR. OBERMAN READ AN EARLY DRAFT OF THE AUTHORS' DESCRIPTION OF THOSE EVENTS, AND HE KINDLY PROVIDED FEEDBACK.

THIS BOOK ALSO BENEFITED FROM THE LIVELY COMMENTS OF JON THOMASON, KEN THOMASON, KATHY HOFF, LOIS SEAVER, DAVID LEV, AND PAMELA D'ANGELO. HOLLY WOULD ESPECIALLY

LIKE TO THANK HER HUSBAND, DAVE TRECHTER, FOR HIS TENDER PATIENCE AND LOVING SUPPORT.

ANY MISTAKES THAT MIGHT EXIST IN THIS BOOK ARE HOLLY'S AND JANE'S.

FINALLY, THE AUTHORS ARE AWESTRUCK BY THE HUNDREDS OF PEOPLE WHO PUT THEIR HEARTS AND SOULS INTO THE GALILEO PROJECT. THEIR WORK ON THIS COMPELLING MISSION CONTINUES TO HUMBLE AND INSPIRE.

CPSIA information can be obtained
at www.ICGtesting.com
Printed in the USA
LVHW071452131020
668698LV00001B/7